A PARENT'S GUIDE TO

INSTAGRAM

Tyndale House Publishers
Carol Stream, Illinois

Visit Tyndale online at tyndale.com.

Visit Axis online at axis.org.

Tyndale and Tyndale's quill logo are registered trademarks of Tyndale House Ministries.

A Parent's Guide to Instagram

For information about special discounts for bulk purchases, please contact Tyndale House Publishers at csresponse@tyndale.com, or call 1-855-277-9400.

Library of Congress Cataloging-in-Publication Data

A catalog record for this book is available from the Library of Congress.

ISBN 978-1-4964-6722-5

Printed in the United States of America

28	27	26	25	24	23	22
7	6	5	4	3	2	1

We need to teach children
how to cope with all aspects of social
media—good and bad—to prepare
them for an increasingly digitized
world. There is real danger in blaming
the medium for the message.

**SIR SIMON WESSELY,
FORMER PRESIDENT, ROYAL COLLEGE
OF PSYCHIATRISTS**

CONTENTS

A LETTER FROM AXIS

Dear Reader,

We're Axis, and since 2007, we've been creating resources to help connect parents, teens, and Jesus in a disconnected world. We're a group of gospel-minded researchers, speakers, and content creators, and we're excited to bring you the best of what we've learned about making meaningful connections with the teens in your life.

This parent's guide is designed to help start a conversation. Our goal is to give you enough knowledge that you're able to ask your teen informed questions about their world. For each guide, we spend weeks reading, researching, and interviewing parents and teens in order to distill everything you need to know about the topic at hand. We encourage you to read the whole thing and then to use the questions we include to get the conversation going with your teen—and then to follow the conversation wherever it leads.

As Douglas Stone, Bruce Patton, and Sheila Heen point out in their book *Difficult Conversations*, "Changes in attitudes and behavior rarely come about because of arguments, facts, and attempts to persuade. How often do *you* change your values and beliefs—or whom you love or what you want in life—based on something someone tells you? And how likely are you to do so when the person who is trying to change you doesn't seem fully aware of the reasons you see things differently in the first place?"[1] For whatever reason, when we believe that others are trying to understand *our* point of view, our defenses usually go down, and we're more willing to listen to *their* point of view. The rising generation is no exception.

So we encourage you to ask questions, to listen, and then to share your heart with your teen. As we often say at Axis, discipleship happens where conversation happens.

Sincerely,
Your friends at Axis

[1] Douglas Stone, Bruce Patton, and Sheila Heen, *Difficult Conversations: How to Discuss What Matters Most*, rev. ed. (New York: Penguin Books, 2010), 137.

INSTANT GRATIFICATION OR A NEVER-ENDING SEARCH FOR VALIDATION?

THOUGH MUCH YOUNGER than its predecessors, Instagram has become a social media behemoth through its simplicity, ease of use, and focus on imagery. Along with Snapchat, it's considered by many teens as a nonnegotiable in their arsenal of online profiles. So what's the good, bad, and ugly of the app? Let's look at how the app is changing us, both for better and worse.

WHAT IS INSTAGRAM?

INSTAGRAM IS A FREE photo-sharing mobile app that was launched in 2010 to inspire creativity through visual storytelling. It quickly gained traction and now has over one billion monthly active users,[1] ranging from celebrities to "influencers" (those with large social media followings) to brands to your average person. Since Facebook bought the company in 2012 for $1 billion, Instagram's growth rate has exponentially increased[2] and about half of its users get on the app daily.[3] Instagram's Stories feature, adapted from Snapchat, now has approximately 500 million daily active users, outpacing the app it was adapted from.[4]

HOW POPULAR IS IT?

INSTAGRAM IS MOST POPULAR among people younger than twenty-five, and those users spend on average more than thirty-two minutes a day on the app. In addition, "statistics show that 20% of all Internet users are on Instagram [, and the] Pew Research Center found that 52% of teens say that Instagram is their favorite social networking site." [5]

"52% of teens say that Instagram is their favorite social networking site."

—PEW RESEARCH CENTER

HOW DOES IT WORK?

AXIS

AT ITS MOST BASIC, the mobile app (for both iOS and Android) allows a user to take/ upload a photo or video, choose whether or not to make edits to the file, add a caption, choose whether or not to share it to their other social media accounts (like Facebook and Twitter), and post it to their profile. Other users who have followed that user will see the post in their feeds and can choose to like (denoted by a heart), comment on, share, bookmark, or report it.

Beyond that, a user can now upload multiple photos or videos in a post, as well as create collages (using Instagram's app Layout).[6] Photos/videos can also be edited and have filters applied within the app. Posts can be edited (only the captions, not the photo itself) or deleted at any point after posting. In addition, a user can tag another user in a post, which

9

causes that post to appear in a tab on the other user's profile. Finally, a user can add his or her location to a post. (This feature is especially important to discuss with teens.) This article explains:

Teens can easily share the location of where they took the picture when they post. This setting allows a user to tag their picture to a particular address or location. If you click on that location once the post is up, the app brings you to a map and a small dot that shows exactly where they were when they took the picture. We saw so many pictures that we were able to easily click on and even see the users' home location or their favorite coffee shop that they just might visit regularly. To ensure safety, follow these directions: Go to your teen's phone settings, select "Instagram," click on "location," select "never."[7]

CAN YOU EXPLAIN ITS IMPORTANT FEATURES?

FOR THOSE WHO HAVE no familiarity with the app, Instagram has five distinct pages, or tabs: your profile, the home feed, the Explore tab, the Reels tab, and a Shop tab. We'll discuss a few of these in more detail below.

PROFILE

A user's profile can be set to either private or public, and, much like other social networks, users can follow other profiles (if the profile is private, they must first be approved by the user before viewing any of their posts).[8] To follow an account, locate the other user by searching for their name or "handle" (aka username; denoted by the @ symbol). For example, @AxisConnection leads to the Axis account. A profile includes the user's profile picture, any personal information the user shares in his or her bio (limited to 150 characters[9]), number of followers, number followed by that account, and, most notably, all the photos/videos the user has posted or been tagged in.

WHAT PARENTS NEED TO KNOW

According to Instagram's Terms of Use[10], the age requirement to use the service is thirteen. This is because of the Children's Online Privacy Protection Act (COPPA), which establishes that websites and online services cannot collect data on children under the age of thirteen without parental consent. If someone younger than thirteen joins Instagram by using a fake birth date during registration for the app, COPPA cannot protect them.

Just because your child is tech-savvy at the age of ten doesn't necessarily mean that he or she is mature enough to use social media sites. It can be difficult for children to truly understand the impact of their online actions (or the impact of actions against them), which can be particularly harmful when it comes to cyberbullies, "trolls," and online predators.

Once your teen is legally old enough to join the service, it's a good idea to make sure their account is private rather than public and to discuss with your teen the issues surrounding online safety and privacy.[11] Teens often don't understand the permanence and potential repercussions of sending information out into the virtual world.

Other conversation topics: The fluidity of online identities. Online profiles make it easy and tempting to "reinvent" ourselves or to project a certain image or persona, even if it's not authentic. It's even

Teens often don't understand the permanence and potential repercussions of sending information out into the virtual world.

common for users to juggle multiple Instagram accounts. There is a big difference between re-creating our image over social media and being transformed into the likeness of Christ—between the biblical concept of "taking off the old self and putting on the new" (see Ephesians 4:22-23) and projecting an identity via social media that might be a far cry from who we actually are and who God calls us to be.

HOME FEED

The **home feed** is the tab where a user can scroll through all the photos/videos posted by accounts a user follows, as well as "sponsored" posts (i.e., ads). The profiles a user follows can be those of other individuals, impersonal accounts (e.g., @cats_of_instagram), or verified accounts of celebrities, influencers, and brands (indicated by a blue check mark).

WHAT PARENTS NEED TO KNOW

Although Instagram traded in Facebook's "Friend" title for Twitter's more ambiguous "Follower" as a way to refer to those with whom a user connects and interacts, it can be easy for teens to scroll through an Instagram home feed and feel as though they are truly connected to those they follow, to believe they have true insight into their lives, whether or not they have real-world interactions with them. However, it's important to make teens aware that, just as they have the ability to project an inauthentic online image and persona, so do those they follow.

Instagram can be a good tool for connection on one level; however, teens also need to realize that they cannot replace their deep, God-given need for real-world community with virtual interactions, which can be a false and unfulfilling

Teens also need to realize that they cannot replace their deep, God-given need for real-world community with virtual interactions, which can be a false and unfulfilling substitute.

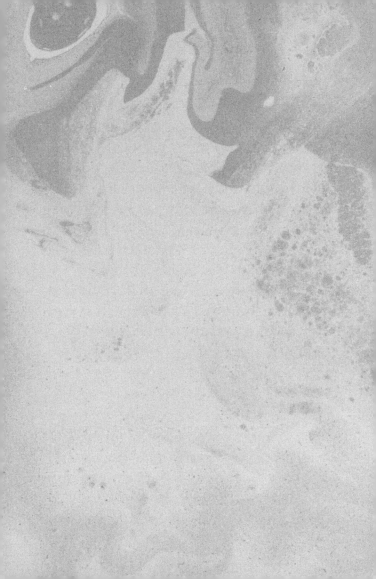

substitute. It's simpler to settle for virtual interactions because they are cognitively and emotionally easier than real-world ones, but easier does not mean better, deeper, or more authentic.[12] Discuss with your teen how he or she can use Instagram as a way to supplement real-world relationships, instead of allowing the app to replace or diminish them.

More information about identity and community in regard to Instagram can be found below in the discussion about Instagram and mental health.

EXPLORE

Instagram's **Explore** (i.e., search) tab was added in 2012. At the top of the tab is a search bar for finding other people and content by entering names, handles, hashtags, words, and phrases. (Note: The app does keep track of a user's search history, but it can easily be cleared.[13]) Below this, the Explore tab uses algorithms to show users a variety of curated content based on location, what's trending, and individual users' interests. This is not content from profiles the user follows; it's content that Instagram algorithmically suggests to the user. Among the thumbnails of photos and other videos, you'll also find videos from the Reels tab. Tapping on any one of them will take you to the Reels section of the Instagram app.

WHAT PARENTS NEED TO KNOW

The quote "Music may not tell you what to think, but it does tell you what to think about" can easily be applied to Instagram. But it may even go a step further, subliminally telling us what to like, as the author of this *New York Times Magazine* article writes:

[Instagram's Explore feature] provides curated randomness—a category that can exist only in an era of algorithms. The distance between what I like and what Instagram thinks I might like is oceanic, preposterous, deranged. And yet the algorithm is not wrong. I press the "like" button on a picture of my friend, and the Explore page shows me albino crocodiles. I comment on a cute dog, and the Explore page offers circus contortionists. Suddenly I like those things, too.[14]

Ads became part of the home feed in 2013. Unlike on Facebook, ads on Instagram are shown regardless of the user's interests, which complements the "curated randomness" of the Explore tab.

Other conversation topics: What does it mean to explore? Instagram defines exploration as something that happens on a screen. How is this different from exploring God's creation through real-world experiences, discovery, and adventures? How can we use Instagram to supplement and complement our real-world experiences, rather than letting it curb innovation and actual exploration?

How can we use
Instagram to supplement
and complement our
real-world experiences,
rather than letting it
curb innovation and
actual exploration?

WHAT ARE HASHTAGS?

AS WITH OTHER social media apps, hashtags (i.e., "#" followed by words and/or numbers) have been an integral part of how Instagram operates since its inception. They are essentially a way to promote a photo, though they can also just be a way to add parenthetical humor (a post-workout photo might be captioned with "#mylegsarekillingme"). For example, captioning a photo with "#fitness" will link that photo to all the other content on the app with the same hashtag. Then when a user searches "#fitness" in the Explore tab (or by tapping on the hashtag when it appears below a photo or video), they are taken to a page with all the posts containing that hashtag.

There are many things to understand when it comes to hashtags. For example, it's common practice for users to caption their content with the most popular hashtags (check out the top 100 at top-hashtags.com/instagram/) in order to gain viewership and followers. In addition, there are many hashtag trends, like hashtags for every day of the week. The hashtag #mcm (Man-Crush Monday) is used to show affection for a significant other or a celebrity one likes (similar to #wcw—Woman-Crush Wednesday). Also, #tbt (Throwback Thursday) and #fbf (Flashback Friday) are paired with a photo from the past, even if that past is as recent as yesterday. Finally, users can now follow hashtags like they follow other users in order to be updated when new content is tagged with that hashtag.

WHAT'S INSTAGRAM DIRECT?

IT'S INSTAGRAM'S VERSION of private messaging, which was launched in 2013 and is denoted by a paper airplane icon. Via Instagram Direct, users are able to send messages containing text, photos, videos, and/or others' posts to one or more users. Like Snapchat, photos and videos sent in this way can be set to disappear immediately after viewing.

It's important to note that users can receive direct messages (DMs) from users whom they have not allowed to follow their private account, and there are methods to save copies of self-destructing, "disappearing" content. In addition, Instagram Direct conversations can be erased.

Other conversation topics: The false security of "private" online interactions; how to decline to view direct messages from unknown users,[15] as well as block and report them.[16] (If you have access to your teen's direct messages and notice a lot of disappearing content, talk to them as to why they choose disappearing over permanent.)

WHAT ARE STORIES?

IN 2016, INSTAGRAM ADDED a Stories feature (adapted from Snapchat, like many of Instagram's features) to its app. This feature allows a user to upload videos and/or photos that disappear after twenty-four hours. If a user has an active story, a colorful rim will appear around their profile picture at the top of the home page. The home feed shows all the profile pictures of users with active stories. Tapping on one of these profile pictures will show that user's picture(s) and/or video(s) depending on how many Stories the user has uploaded in the last twenty-four hours. The content can be viewed as many times as desired before it disappears. In addition, users can now livestream themselves and their experiences in real time via their Stories, a feature that was added later in 2016.

WHY WOULD SOMEONE WANT TO POST TO THEIR STORY INSTEAD OF TO THEIR PROFILE?

INSTAGRAM WAS ORIGINALLY MEANT to be an app for instant photo and video sharing of immediately present moments (hence the prefix "insta-"). Over time, users instead began sharing photos outside of the present moment—photos of moments that had happened previously and were then edited. Initially, these photos were often captioned with the hashtag #latergram to indicate that they were not true *insta*grams. However, this caption is now usually left off altogether, as users' profiles (and, as a result, Instagram itself) have become more about artistry, photography, and edited content. Users, generally speaking, no longer want to post those blurry, spontaneous, insta-photos.

However, Instagram's adaptation of Snapchat's Stories feature combats this and provides users with the means to maintain the spontaneous, insta-sharing nature of the app, while still having the option to post artistic, edited, more professional-looking photos to their profiles—photos which are more permanent in that they do not automatically disappear but, rather, can only be manually deleted. The Stories feature tends to promote authenticity rather than the "highlight reel" nature of the regular, often highly edited posts.

Other conversation topics: The false security that the "disappearing" content lends itself to; how to keep personal information private and out of one's Story; the need to be aware and cautious of what is said and done over livestream. (As an example, one Instagram influencer accidentally livestreamed herself having sex with her boyfriend. **What happens live cannot be taken back.**)

IS INSTAGRAM ART?

FOR MANY, INSTAGRAM is a platform for artistic, creative expression. In her fascinating TED talk, Jia Jia Fei discusses Instagram's impact on art standards and the entire art world.[17] Art standards are becoming more relative and subjective. Now everyone is a photographer. Instagram, other social media sites/apps, and the internet as a whole are also contributing to changing art standards by replacing museums as the art authority. Fei talks about how the way we experience art has changed through the digitization of images. However, she ends her presentation on a hopeful note by calling on museums to cross over into the digital space, reclaim their authority in the art world, and utilize apps like Instagram for engagement and education.

Conversation starter: Watch Fei's TED talk with your teen, then discuss the topics she covers and questions she poses during her presentation. How can we keep creativity and artistic expression via Instagram from becoming more about convenience than quality?

WHAT'S A "FINSTA"?

SHORT FOR "FAKE INSTAGRAM," these are second (or third or fourth) accounts that teens have either to get away from the prying eyes of concerned adults or simply to enjoy a pressure-free account in which they're unconcerned about posting the perfect shot or getting lots of likes.[18] While the latter reason is understandable, the former is what's concerning. Teens who have Finstas for this reason often want a place to post pictures they don't want their parents to see.

While many of us are quick to think that our kids would never do that, it doesn't hurt to ask. When doing so, simply be calm and ask if they have a Finsta. If they admit to it, gently move into questions about why they feel the need to have one, if you can see it, etc. If they say they don't, they may be telling the truth! Either way, make sure to remind them that they can tell you anything, that you're there for them, and that you want what's best for them.

WHY DO TEENS CARE SO MUCH ABOUT HOW MANY FOLLOWERS AND LIKES THEY GET?

LARGELY (IF NOT EXCLUSIVELY) BECAUSE of hashtags, one of the primary focuses of using social media apps like Instagram has become self-promotion. It's the new way to build a brand and a business around one's passion. Some of the most recognized celebrities and influencers (like Kim Kardashian, for example) now exclusively advertise their products over social media. Beyond that, though, many regular teens want to gain a following and become influencers. Why? It's validating, and it's the new fast track to fame and significance.

In essence, one's number of followers, likes, and views has come to represent one's social value. The more followers and likes, the more popular—and valuable—a person is. In fact, most Gen Zers care less about being invited to parties or having lots of friends at school and much, much more about their number of

One's number of followers, likes, and views has come to represent one's social value. The more followers and likes, the more popular—and valuable—a person is.

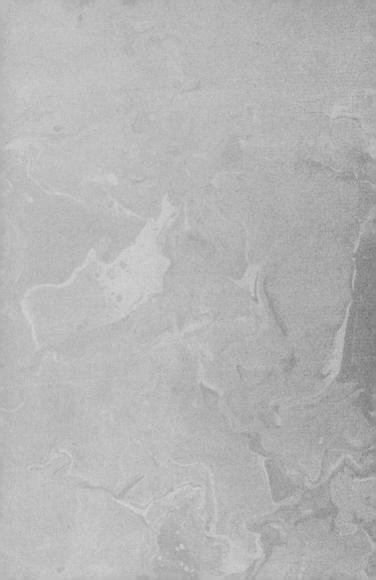

followers, their "Snap Scores," how many positive comments they get, etc.[19] So if your teen happens to be obsessing over their numbers, this is likely why.

Developmentally this all makes sense. Teens are especially preoccupied with identity and ego at this stage in their life. It's not anything bad; in fact, it's age appropriate. They are learning who they are, what makes them unique, and what makes them special. But if they continue to seek significance or validation from others instead of finding their inherent worth as Christ's beloved, their thirst for external significance will never be quenched.

Other conversation topics: What are your reasons for wanting an Instagram account? Could there be an element of self-promotion and/or validation? Or is there another, greater purpose? What would it look like to use your profile for positive influence? What do you think happens to a person when they are valued for their "numbers"? Do you think your social following is a true reflection of who you are and your value? How does this mentality line up with what God says about our worth and value?

HOW DO THE LIKING AND COMMENTING FEATURES AFFECT MY TEEN?

THE VALIDATION of having someone else like or leave an encouraging comment on your content is a form of positive reinforcement, which releases serotonin. And the unpredictability of whether or not feedback will be positive is what makes social media addiction a real phenomenon. Shirley Cramer, chief executive of the Royal Society for Public Health (RSPH), says, "Social media has been described as more addictive than cigarettes and alcohol, and is now so entrenched in the lives of young people that it is no longer possible to ignore it when talking about young people's mental health issues."[20]

Ironically, if a teen has a public account, chances are many of the comments he or she receives are posted by a "bot"— basically, a program that goes on "liking, following, and commenting sprees" as a "rogue marketing tactic meant to catch the attention of other Instagram users in hopes that they will follow or like the automated accounts in return."[21]

Bob Gilbreath, chief executive of Ahalogy (a marketing technology company in Cincinnati), explains: "The follower count is really completely meaningless. It's untrustworthy for the true following, and it's certainly untrustworthy for the quality of the creative work." Calder Wilson, a professional photographer, says, "When you have [a bot] coming in there and leaving fake comments like 'stunning photo' and 'stunning gallery' and there's no one behind it and then the likes—it's as if they hijacked that personal neuropathway in your brain."[22]

For teens who are even more vulnerable to this type of "hijacking," getting more likes, comments, and followers can be exhilarating and validating. But the opposite is also true: when they don't receive the numbers they were hoping to get on a post, they will often feel rejected, unloved, and unwanted. Many will remove posts if they don't perform as desired.

We can protect teens from this kind of false commenting simply by ensuring that their accounts are kept private and are unable to be accessed by random accounts. However, simply requiring that our teens keep their accounts private without any explanation will do us and them no good. We must help them understand why we require this, which means having loving conversations about validation, worth, fame, friendship, comparison, and much more. If we skip these conversations, this will only serve to alienate our kids, and if they're determined enough, they will find ways around our rules.

To help protect teens from cyberbullying via comments (and this applies whether a teen has a private account or a public one), Instagram rolled out a tool that allows users to block comments containing specific keywords,[23] and also introduced a feature that allows users to disable comments completely on individual posts.[24]

HOW DOES THE APP IMPACT MY TEEN'S MENTAL HEALTH?

A STUDY CALLED #STATUSOFMIND, published in the UK by the RSPH's Young Health Movement, examined the positive and negative effects of social media platforms on the mental health of young people. It revealed that Instagram is the worst app for young people's mental health. The 1,479 fourteen- to twenty-four-year-olds polled were asked to rate five different social media platforms—YouTube, Twitter, Facebook, Snapchat, and Instagram—on fourteen different issues, including anxiety, depression, loneliness, sleep (the quality and amount), body image, bullying, and FOMO (fear of missing out). Instagram received the worst marks on every issue. (The other social media platforms were ranked in the order given above, with YouTube being the most positive.) Instagram was most positively rated on self-expression (the expression of your feelings, thoughts, and ideas) and

Instagram is the worst app for young people's mental health.

self-identity (ability to define who you are). But, as previously discussed, conversations need to happen even around these "positively rated" issues.

Instagram and other social media platforms can also lure users into comparison (with other users by viewing their posts and content), which can lead to feelings of inadequacy and envy—commonly referred to as "Facebook envy." Not coincidentally, the two worst-ranked platforms—Snapchat and Instagram—are both image-focused.[25]

Hanna Krasnova, coauthor of a study on Facebook and envy, says, "A photo can very powerfully provoke immediate social comparison, and that can trigger feelings of inferiority. . . . If you see beautiful photos of your friend on Instagram, one way to compensate is to self-present with even better photos, and then your friend sees your photos and posts *even better* photos, and so on. *Self-promotion triggers more self-promotion, and the world on social media gets further and further from reality*" (emphasis added).[26]

The #StatusOfMind study found this issue of comparison most prevalent among young women in regard to body image. The author of the report explains that Instagram draws young women into comparison by promoting "unrealistic, largely curated, filtered and Photoshopped versions of reality."[27] A hundred years ago, a young woman likely had only a small pool of others to compare herself to: those in her local community. Now young women are throwing their posts and self-images up against unlimited numbers of others. This is new territory.

However, Sir Simon Wessely, former president of the UK's Royal College of Psychiatrists, encourages educating young people about how to use social media platforms *well*, rather than demonizing social media. He says, "I am sure that social media plays a role in unhappiness, but it has as many benefits as it does negatives. We need to teach children how to cope with all aspects of social media—good and bad—to prepare them for an increasingly digitized world. *There is real danger in blaming the medium for the message*" (emphasis added).[28]

We need to teach children how to cope with all aspects of social media— good and bad—to prepare them for an increasingly digitized world.

HOW DO I TALK TO MY TEENS ABOUT COMPARISON AND BODY IMAGE?

A TREND IS GAINING MOMENTUM to combat comparison and the unrealistic standards that young women have been attempting to attain for so long. The forerunners of this movement include Tess Holliday, Lena Dunham, and Ashley Graham—all celebrities and influencers with huge followings on Instagram. Phrases like "body love," "self love," "love yourself," and "love the skin you're in" are often attached to this movement. Tess Holliday, who is involved more in the online aspect of the movement, calls it BoPo—short for "body positive." Body positivity is ultimately about embracing the normalcy of all body types and characteristics, not just those traditionally labeled as beautiful, and about "opening the door" to those who have disabilities, disorders, and stereotypically un-beautiful appearances in a way that "transcends language" and is "visual [in] nature."[29] These influencers, as well as Claire Mysko, the chief executive of National Eating Disorders Association, encourage Instagram users to curate their feeds and online experiences to that end.

But this is tricky. The body positivity movement is meant to combat an area of our culture that desperately needs to be addressed and changed—the unrealistic standards of physical beauty and the constant attack on young people's self-worth—but the cultural answer to this problem rings hollow (and can even promote narcissism) because it's still based on externals. Sure, it changes the conversation to broaden our perspective on beauty, but in the end, the body positivity movement finds our intrinsic worth in our bodies rather than in Christ.

If the identity and worth of human beings—and, in this context, specifically young women—is completely dependent upon God's identity and the worth He's given us, how can we adequately create change in this area apart from Him? What the body positivity movement offers is only a shadow of the abundant life and secure identity that God desires for young women. We must affirm to our teenage daughters that worth is not something they have to fight to assert and assign to themselves (as the body positivity movement often encourages them to do); it is already intrinsic to who they are *because of* who God is and *who He says they are*. Identity is not meant to be self-assigned but, rather, divinely authored.

As parents, it's also important that we confirm God's truth about our teenage daughters through words of validation and affirmation. Young women may be less inclined to seek that validation from

Identity is not meant to be self-assigned but, rather, divinely authored.

social media or be made insecure by what they're exposed to there if they are edified and their God-given worth affirmed within the home.

Pay attention to the accounts your teenage daughter follows and notice if any of them have a disproportionate number of selfies, especially revealing ones. Ultimately, the body positivity movement fights a negative emphasis on physical appearance with a positive emphasis on physical appearance. However, biblically, our emphasis should not be on the physical at all. "Your beauty should not come from outward adornment. . . . Rather, it should be that of your inner self, the unfading beauty of a gentle and quiet spirit, which is of great worth in God's sight" (1 Peter 3:3-4). Guiding teenage daughters into confidence and security in their physical appearance and helping them to recognize their God-given worth—while also teaching them to value even more the fashioning of their character—cannot adequately be addressed in this guide (nor is that the primary purpose of it). However, there are other helpful resources for starting this conversation with your teenage daughter, which we'll share at the end of this guide.

CAN A USER ACCESS INAPPROPRIATE CONTENT ON THE APP?

INSTAGRAM DESIRES TO FOSTER a positive environment and has strict community guidelines and policies against inappropriate and sexually explicit content. Public content is moderated by Instagram and can be reported as inappropriate by other users and subsequently removed by the company.

That being said, teens can quickly learn hashtags and secret emoji codes that will direct them to explicit content. Certain hashtags have been used for the illegal sale of drugs, and porn is often hidden under foreign-language hashtags.

Instagram has combated users' attempts to circumvent their policies regarding explicit content by implementing two different strategies: a "hard ban" and a "soft ban." A hard ban means that a hashtag will return no results (for example, searching for #porn yields no results), whereas a soft ban means that certain images will be prevented from appearing under a hashtag.[30] Other content is viewable but with a warning and an option to get help. For example, searching the hashtag #thinspo or #thinspiration will result in a pop-up that warns the user that he/she is searching a hashtag often linked with self-harm and allows him/her to choose to "Show Posts" or "Get Support."

In an article about how to get around explicit content filters, the writer points out, "Instagram's strict community guidelines on nudity and aggressive band of content moderators mean that most of the really titillating stuff has a relatively short shelf life. The term 'Instaporn' now has a double meaning: it's porn that's gone in an instant."[31]

So although there *is* sexually explicit content on the app, Instagram typically makes it difficult enough to find and view the content that it's not worth the effort when it's so readily available elsewhere. A more legitimate reason for concern may be the content that can be privately shared between users via "disappearing" photos and videos.

HOW DO I TALK TO MY TEENS ABOUT THE APP AND ITS PLACE IN THEIR LIVES?

OPEN-ENDED DISCUSSIONS

Allow their interest in and use of Instagram to be an ongoing but balanced conversation (it might not be a good idea to comment on *everything* they post). Let them know that you are a safe place to go when they experience struggles with or need wisdom about social media. If you allow your teen to have an Instagram account, consider setting up one for yourself as well so you can better monitor their activity, relate to them, and interact with them in the digital spaces they occupy.

ACCOUNTABILITY AND BOUNDARIES

If you choose to allow your teen to have an Instagram account, he/she will need your guidance and wisdom to interact with this social media app *well*. Establishing boundaries and accountability is part of this. Instagram does not have any parental controls within the app, but you can download software to monitor (to some extent) your teen's use of the app. Some of these programs are listed in the resources section at the end of this guide.

One of these software programs, Qustodio, allows parents to monitor *how much* time teens spend on social media apps. This is important because, according to the #StatusOfMind study, "young people who . . . [spend] more than two hours per day on social networking sites such as Facebook, Twitter, or Instagram . . . are more likely to report poor mental health, including psychological distress."[32] Setting boundaries around how much time teens spend on different social media platforms can guard them against the addictive nature of those

"Young people who . . . [spend] more than two hours per day on social networking sites such as Facebook, Twitter, or Instagram . . . are more likely to report poor mental health, including psychological distress."

—#STATUSOFMIND STUDY

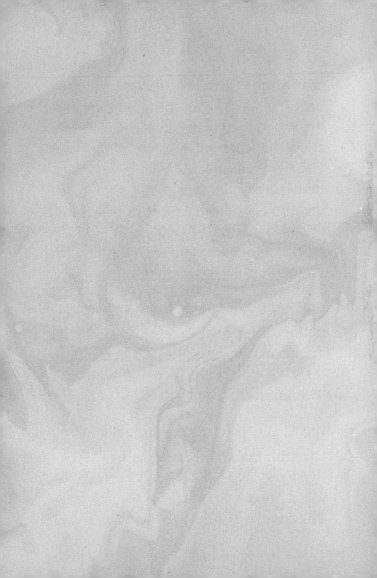

platforms. Qustodio also allows parents the ability to set certain hours during which their teen can access different social media apps (for example, only from 5 to 6 p.m., after school hours but before dinnertime). Qustodio can also block certain apps from being downloaded, and it can disable your teen's phone completely—except for calls—during set times (like during the night).

Another strategy is to turn off Instagram notifications so that teens do not feel compelled to enter the app every time they are notified of activity related to their account.

Finally, consider and discuss with your teen the benefits of occasionally "fasting" from Instagram. Taking intermittent social media breaks is a way to create space in our lives to reprioritize and self-evaluate—and to remind ourselves that social media apps can be *useful tools*, but they are not our source of life, value, identity, or joy.

CONCLUSION

INSTAGRAM IS NOT INHERENTLY EVIL. Whether or not we decide to allow our teens to use Instagram (which is a personal parenting decision based on each teen and their journey), ultimately we need to educate our kids about how to have wisdom in today's culture.

As one of our readers once said to us, "Don't live your life to make an impression; live your life to make an impact." Instagram can easily become about making a good impression—about comparing and competing with our highlight reels. But how can we encourage our teens to use this app as *one way* in which they can have an impact? How can we encourage them to use Instagram in ways that are others-focused—to give, encourage, influence, and impact—instead of ways that seek to *get* validation, entertainment, escape, etc.? How can they *utilize*

Instagram (instead of letting the app control *them*) as a platform for positive influence?

Ultimately, we want to raise our kids to passionately pursue the best life God has for them. We don't do that by allowing them to do whatever they want whenever they want, nor by banning everything and explaining nothing. Rather, we do that by discipling, conversing with, and loving them, always guiding them toward the high-but-fulfilling standards God has set.

ADDITIONAL RESOURCES

1. "Creating a Social Media Contract for Students": http://www.youthministry media.ca/creating-a-social-media -contract-for-students/

2. "The Social Media Contract That Will Get You and Your Kids Talking": https:// lindastade.com/useful-social-media -contract/

3. Bark, an app for tracking texting and social media activity

4. Circle, a device that helps put healthy boundaries on device activity

5. Qustodio, an app for tracking and limiting time spent online

6. Screentime, an app for tracking and limiting time spent online

7. Connect Safely: https://www .connectsafely.org/

8. Defend Young Minds: https://www .defendyoungminds.com/

9. The Online Mom: https://www .theonlinemom.com/

NOTES

1. Brian Dean, "Instagram Demographic Statistics: How Many People Use Instagram in 2022?" Backlinko, January 5, 2022, https://backlinko.com/instagram-users.

2. "Number of Instagram Users Worldwide from 2019 to 2023," Statista, accessed April 24, 2022, https://www.statista.com/statistics/183585/instagram-number-of-global-users/.

3. Brian Dean, "Instagram Demographic Statistics: How Many People Use Instagram in 2022?" Backlinko, January 5, 2022, https://backlinko.com/instagram-users.

4. Dean, "Instagram Demographic Statistics."

5. "5 Uncomfortable Facts about Instagram Every Parent Should Know," Netsanity, February 22, 2017, https://netsanity.net/instagram-parents-info/.

6. Layout from Instagram, App Store, accessed March 13, 2022, https://apps.apple.com/us/app/layout-from-instagram/id967351793.

7. "5 Uncomfortable Facts about Instagram," Netsanity.

8. "Editing Your Profile," Instagram Help Center, accessed March 13, 2022, https://help .instagram.com/448523408565555.

9. Jacqueline Zote, "How Long Should Social Posts Be? Try This Social Media Character Counter," Sprout Social, July 26, 2021, https:// sproutsocial.com/insights/social-media -character-counter/.

10. "Terms of Use," Instagram Help Center, accessed March 13, 2022, https://help .instagram.com/478745558852511.

11. "Editing Your Profile," Instagram Help Center.

12. Liraz Margalit, "The Psychology behind Social Media Interactions," *Psychology Today*, August 29, 2014, https://www.psychologytoday .com/us/blog/behind-online-behavior /201408/the-psychology-behind-social -media-interactions.

13. "Search and Explore," Instagram Help Center, accessed March 13, 2022, https://help .instagram.com/354860134605952.

14. Molly Young, "Letter of Recommendation: Instagram Explore," *New York Times Magazine*, January 5, 2017, https://www.nytimes.com/2017/01/05/magazine/letter-of-recommendation-instagram-explore.html.

15. "Direct Messaging," Instagram Help Center, accessed March 13, 2022, https://help.instagram.com/561290520611666.

16. "Direct Messaging," Instagram Help Center.

17. Jia Jia Fei, "Art in the Age of Instagram," TEDx Talks, video, 13:23, March 2, 2016, https://www.youtube.com/watch?v=8DLNFDQt8Pc.

18. Caity Weaver and Danya Issawi, "'Finsta,' Explained," *New York Times*, September 30, 2021, https://www.nytimes.com/2021/09/30/style/finsta-instagram-accounts-senate.html.

19. Jean M. Twenge, "Why Teens Aren't Partying Anymore," *Wired*, December 27, 2017, https://www.wired.com/story/why-teens-arent-partying-anymore/.

20. "Instagram Ranked Worst for Young People's Mental Health," Royal Society for Public Health, May 19, 2017, https://www.rsph.org

.uk/about-us/news/instagram-ranked-worst
-for-young-people-s-mental-health.html.

21. Sapna Maheshwari, "How Bots Are Inflating
    Instagram Egos," *New York Times*, June 6,
    2017, https://www.nytimes.com/2017/06/06
    /business/media/instagram-bots.html.

22. Maheshwari, "How Bots Are Inflating
    Instagram Egos."

23. Anthony Bouchard, "How to Filter Comments
    in Instagram Based on Keywords," iDB, March
    2, 2021, https://www.idownloadblog
    .com/2016/09/13/how-to-filter-comments-in
    -instagram-based-on-keywords/.

24. "Privacy Settings & Information," Instagram
    Help Center, accessed March 13, 2022, https://
    help.instagram.com/1766818986917552.

25. "#StatusofMind," Royal Society for Public
    Health, accessed March 13, 2022, https://
    www.rsph.org.uk/our-work/campaigns/status
    -of-mind.html.

26. "5 Uncomfortable Facts about Instagram,"
    Netsanity.

27. Kara Fox, "Instagram Worst Social Media App

for Young People's Mental Health," CNN Health, May 19, 2017, https://www.cnn.com/2017/05/19/health/instagram-worst-social-network-app-young-people-mental-health/index.html.

28. Fox, "Instagram Worst Social Media App."

29. Maya Salam, "Why 'Radical Body Love' Is Thriving on Instagram," *New York Times*, June 9, 2017, https://www.nytimes.com/2017/06/09/style/body-positive-instagram.html.

30. Sam Hackett, "A Complete List of Banned Hashtags You Should Avoid in 2022," Kicksta, November 19, 2021, https://blog.kicksta.co/a-complete-list-of-banned-hashtags-you-should-avoid/.

31. Amrita Khalid and John-Michael Bond, "The Sneaky Way to Find Hidden NSFW Content on Instagram," Daily Dot, updated August 18, 2021, https://www.dailydot.com/nsfw/guides/porn-on-instagram/.

32. "#StatusofMind," Royal Society for Public Health. See the report at https://www.rsph.org.uk/static/uploaded/d125b27c-0b62-41c5-a2c0155a8887cd01.pdf.

PARENT'S GUIDES
BY AXIS

It's common to feel lost in your teen's world. These pocket-sized guides are packed with clear explanations of teen culture to equip you to have open conversations with your teen, one tough topic at a time. Look for more parent's guides coming soon!

BUNDLE THESE 5 BOOKS AND SAVE

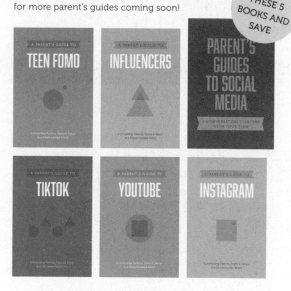

A PARENT'S GUIDE TO
TEEN FOMO
Connecting Parents, Teens & Jesus in a Disconnected World

A PARENT'S GUIDE TO
INFLUENCERS
Connecting Parents, Teens & Jesus in a Disconnected World

PARENT'S GUIDES TO SOCIAL MEDIA
5 CONVERSATION STARTERS WITH YOUR TEEN

A PARENT'S GUIDE TO
TIKTOK
Connecting Parents, Teens & Jesus in a Disconnected World

A PARENT'S GUIDE TO
YOUTUBE
Connecting Parents, Teens & Jesus in a Disconnected World

A PARENT'S GUIDE TO
INSTAGRAM
Connecting Parents, Teens & Jesus in a Disconnected World

DISCOVER MORE PARENT'S GUIDES, VIDEOS, AND AUDIOS AT AXIS.ORG

axis
www.axis.org

CP1805